THE LIFE & TIMES OF
A DOG LOVER

PHOTOGRAPHS BY
BEV SPARKS

HARVEST HOUSE PUBLISHERS

EUGENE, OREGON

THE LIFE AND TIMES OF A DOG LOVER

Text Copyright © 2009 by Harvest House Publishers
Artwork Copyright © by Bev Sparks by arrangement with The Greeting Place

Published by Harvest House Publishers
Eugene, Oregon 97402
www.harvesthousepublishers.com

Text written and compiled by Hope Lyda

ISBN 978-0-7369-2605-8

Design and production by Koechel Peterson & Associates, Inc., Minneapolis, Minnesota

Harvest House Publishers has made every effort to trace the ownership of all poems and quotes. In the event of a question arising from the use of a poem or quote, we regret any error made and will be pleased to make the necessary correction in future editions of this book.

Printed in China

09 10 11 12 13 14 15 / LP / 10 9 8 7 6 5 4 3 2 1

For many of us, love for creation deepens through the relationships we form with our pets, particularly our dogs. By their very nature and need, dogs draw us out of ourselves: they root us in nature, making us more conscious of the mystery of God inherent in all things.

**THE MONKS OF
NEW SKETE**

My little dog— a heartbeat at my feet.

EDITH WHARTON

Until one has loved an animal, a part of one's soul remains unawakened.

ANATOLE FRANCE

DOG LOVERS' CORNER

HE WON the Nobel prize for literature for his travelogue *Travels with Charley.* That's John Steinbeck...and Charley was his French standard poodle, whose full name was Charles le Chien. This duo traveled across America as Steinbeck explored and recorded the state of "American life." The book explores an America that challenges Steinbeck's expectations in many ways, and it also reveals an endearing account of a man and his best friend having an adventure of a lifetime.

All things bright
and beautiful,
all creatures
great and small,
all things wise
and wonderful,
the Lord God
made them all.

CECIL FRANCIS ALEXANDER

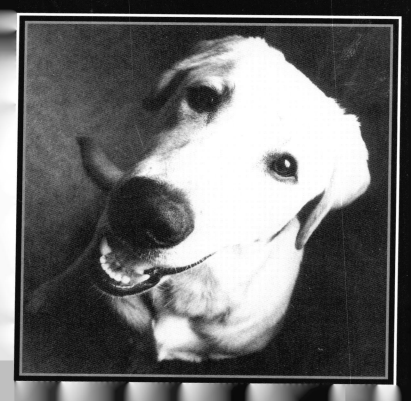

WHY WE LOVE OUR DOGS

DOGS CAN'T WEAR their heart on their sleeve, but they do show their love, zaniness, and intentions on their face. Before they leap across a room to attack a throw pillow or swipe the last piece of chicken from your unprotected plate, their eyes light up. For a split second, they convey their full confession—*before* the crazy act—in their expression.

I TALK TO HIM when I'm lonesome like;

and I'm sure he understands.

When he looks at me so attentively,

and gently licks my hands;

Then he rubs his nose on my tailored clothes,

but I never say naught there at.

For the good Lord knows I can buy more clothes,

but never a friend like that.

W. DAYTON WEDGEFARTH

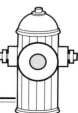

The better I get
to know men, the
more I find myself
loving dogs.

CHARLES DE GAULLE

DOG LOVERS' CORNER

CELEBRATED ACTRESS and humanitarian Audrey Hepburn had a compassionate heart for people and for animals. Her Yorkshire terrier named "Mr. Famous" even got in on her film career action. He starred as the dog in the basket during the train shot in *Anna Karenina.*

No one appreciates the very special genius of your conversation as the dog does.

CHRISTOPHER MORLEY

Children and dogs are as necessary to the welfare of the country as Wall Street and the railroads.

HARRY S. TRUMAN

WHY WE LOVE OUR DOGS

COUNSELOR IN SESSION! Our poor dogs just want a bowlful of treats; instead, they get an earful of our musings, complaints, quandaries, questions, and occasionally our latest, greatest invention concepts. They merely want to cuddle up next to us on the couch; instead, they become our emotional outlet so that we don't have to visit the counselor's couch. We humans have the most discreet and faithful listeners at our sides. They never judge. They always forgive. Be sure to throw a few good words to your favorite listener: walk, car ride, treat, bone, nap, play, friend.

We long for an affection altogether ignorant of our faults. Heaven has accorded this to us in the uncritical canine attachment.

GEORGE ELIOT

MY HOME IS A HAVEN for one who enjoys
The clamour of children and ear-splitting noise
From a number of dogs who are always about,
And who want to come in and, once in, to go out.
Whenever I settle to read by the fire,
Some dog will develop an urge to retire,
And I'm constantly opening and shutting the door
For a dog to depart or, as mentioned before,
For a dog to arrive, who, politely admitted,
Will make a bee-line for the chair I've just quitted.
Our friends may be dumb, but my house is a riot,
Where I cannot sit still and can never be quiet.

RALPH WOTHERSPOON

DOG LOVERS' CORNER

GENERAL PATTON was well-known for having bull terriers as sidekicks. He purchased the last one in 1944, the year before his death. He named the dog Willie, short for "William the Conqueror," and the two were seen together often. Patton wrote in his diary, "My bull pup...took to me like a duck to water."

In order to really enjoy a dog, one doesn't merely try to train him to be semi-human. The point of it is to open oneself to the possibility of becoming partly a dog.

EDWARD HOAGLAND

No man can be condemned for owning a dog. As long as he has a dog, he has a friend; and the poorer he gets, the better friend he has.

WILL ROGERS

WHY WE LOVE OUR DOGS

WHAT DOG isn't a walking, breathing three-ring circus act? They don't need a crowd. In fact, an audience of one very attentive owner or bystander will do. First it's the wiggle, then the ol' peek-a-boo paw over the eyes trick, followed by a sheepish beg, and the finale…the drop-flop-and-roll move. Eager to please, dogs are entertainers at heart. If only they could take their show on the road!

EVERY TIME I told my cocker spaniel, Taffy, my very first dog, that we were going for a walk, she would launch into a celebratory dance that ended with her racing around the room, always clockwise, and faster and faster, as if her joy could not be possibly contained. Even as a young boy I knew that hardly any creature could express joy so vividly as a dog.

JEFFREY MOUSSAIEFF MASSON

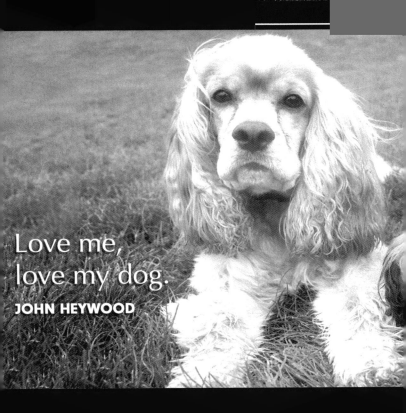

Love me,
love my dog.

JOHN HEYWOOD

DOG LOVERS' CORNER

BOB BARKER has the perfect name to be an advocate for dogs! This beloved game show host for *The Price Is Right* used his high profile to encourage viewers to have their pets spayed and neutered. He also influenced the show to become more animal friendly by eliminating the practice of offering fur coats as prizes. Bob Barker also started the DJ and T Foundation to provide grant funding for clinics offering spaying and neutering services to pet owners.

'TIS SWEET to hear the watch-dog's honest bark

Bay deep-mouthed welcome as we draw near home;

'Tis sweet to know there is an eye will mark

Our coming, and look brighter when we come.

LORD BYRON

The best thing about a man is his dog.

FRENCH PROVERB

WHY WE LOVE OUR DOGS

SUPERDOG! A courageous canine doesn't need a cape to be a hero. There are countless news stories and even more personal stories about dogs of every breed protecting children from harm, returning to burning barns to lead out livestock, jumping into rough waters to save their owners, and braving storms to make their way back home. But it doesn't take a disaster for the truth to come out…our dog companions save us every day with their daring acts of love and loyalty.

I used to look at [my dog] Smokey and think, "If you were a little smarter you could tell me what you were thinking," and he'd look at me like he was saying, "If you were a little smarter, I wouldn't have to."

FRED JUNGCLAUS

Dogs are our link to paradise. They don't know evil or jealousy or discontent. To sit with a dog on a hillside on a glorious afternoon is to be back in Eden, where doing nothing was not boring—it was peace.

MILAN KUNDERA

CESAR MILLAN, known as the "Dog Whisperer," grew to love animals and to explore the basics of leading dogs by watching his grandfather, who was a farmer in Mexico. Millan's love for dogs is evident whether he is writing a book, doing his television show, or working with private clients and their dogs. He started his dog training business with the foundation of a strong work ethic and a desire to help dog owners and their dogs cohabit more happily. His reputation grew, and soon Cesar had a growing clientele. His dream of helping dogs and people became a reality.

BY AND BY came my little puppy, and then my cup was full, my happiness was perfect. It was the dearest little waddling thing, and so smooth and soft and velvety, and had such cunning little awkward paws, and such affectionate eyes, and such a sweet and innocent face; and it made me so proud to see how the children and their mother adored it, and fondled it, and exclaimed over every little wonderful thing it did.

MARK TWAIN
A Dog's Tale

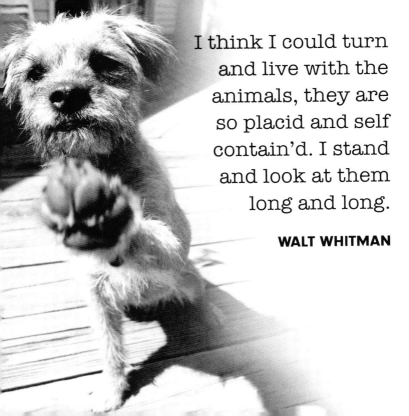

I think I could turn and live with the animals, they are so placid and self contain'd. I stand and look at them long and long.

WALT WHITMAN

WHY WE LOVE OUR DOGS

DOGS ARE THE BEST piece of exercise equipment we can own. When they grab the leash in their mouth and stroll over to where we sit, they transform into our personal trainer—determined and focused. When they trot outside, in any kind of weather, and celebrate the opportunity to breathe in fresh air, they become our cheerleaders, encouraging us to go farther, appreciate more, and worry less. Best of all, you won't need an infomercial to sell you on the benefits of spending quality time with your best friend.

They were loyal little companions, these pets of twenty years; and as I think of the many miles along life's highway that they pattered at my side, making brighter the hours by graceful prank and unfailing love, I breathe a sigh in memory of my dogs, who were my faithful little friends.

CLARA MORRIS
"My Dogs," *The Ladies' Home Journal,* September 1902

It was Toto that made Dorothy laugh, and saved her from growing as gray as her other surroundings.

L. FRANK BAUM
The Wizard of Oz

DOG LOVERS' CORNER

Who doesn't love the droll sense of humor and the amazing fantasies imagined by the dog known worldwide—Snoopy! What some might not realize is that the cartoon version of this cherished dog is based on artist Charles Schulz's childhood dog Spike. No wonder there is such affection for this complex, lovable comic strip character.

Old dogs, like old shoes, are comfortable.
They might be a bit out of shape and a little
worn around the edges, but they fit well.

BONNIE WILCOX

He cannot be a gentleman which loveth not a dog.

JOHN NORTH BROOKE

WHY WE LOVE OUR DOGS

MOST DOG OWNERS would agree that even their untrained canine pals are actually Seeing Eye dogs. When a dog is welcomed into your family, they bring the gift of new vision with them. Suddenly you see dog parks and stretches of grass that you never noticed before. You see opportunities to set aside work and play a little. You witness the satisfaction to be found in throwing an old tennis ball for an hour. And you learn to watch for the moments of joy that each day fetches.

The biggest problem with dogs is that they don't live long enough. They always seem to leave us when we're most vulnerable, most in need of their biased, affirming presence. Dogs make us believe we can actually be as they see us, and it's often only when they're gone that we realize their role in what we've become.

THE MONKS OF NEW SKETE

A house is not a home
until it has a dog.

GERALD DURRELL

DOG LOVERS' CORNER

THE STAR of the movie *Clueless*, Alicia Silverstone, is an avid dog lover and rescuer. She and her husband currently reside with a pack of five rescued dogs, one of which is a Rottweiler/pit bull/Doberman mix she found injured and bleeding in East L.A. while she was filming a movie.

Alicia is a spokesperson for PETA (People for the Ethical Treatment of Animals), but her efforts reach beyond just talking about the importance of caring for our furry friends. She also opened StoneHaven, an animal shelter on her seaside estate.

A dog will make eye contact. A cat will, too, but a cat's eyes don't even look entirely warm-blooded to me, whereas a dog's eyes look human except less guarded. A dog will look at you as if to say, "What do you want me to do for you? I'll do anything for you." Whether a dog can, in fact, do anything for you if you don't have sheep (I never have) is another matter. The dog is willing.

ROY BLOUNT

They are better than human beings because they know but do not tell.

EMILY DICKINSON

DOG LOVERS' CORNER

MARY TYLER MOORE has always had a heart for all animals. And as her celebrity grew, she used her fame to encourage others to treat animals with respect and love. She is the cofounder of Broadway Barks, which is a New York–based annual adopt-a-thon. She also campaigns to promote the adoption of animals from shelters.

The great pleasure of a dog is that you may make a fool of yourself with him and not only will he not scold you but he will make a fool of himself too.

SAMUEL BUTLER

A dog makes the atmosphere safe for emotions, for the expression of the feelings that flow within us. Whatever you're feeling, you can express around your dog. You don't have to censor yourself around your dog as you do around others.

DR. MARTY BECKER

DOG LOVERS' CORNER

ONE OF THE most loved actresses of all time is the beautiful and charming Doris Day. Each movie she starred in seemed to further her career, but behind the scenes her personal efforts furthered a cause beyond celebrity—the care and protection of animals. She founded the Doris Day Animal League and the Doris Day Animal Foundation, which provide education about fair animal treatment and promote awareness of animal welfare issues at the state and federal level. Many dog owners also reap the benefit of Doris Day's hospitality; she co-owns the beautiful Cypress Inn in Carmel, California, which welcomes travelers' dogs and cats.

No matter how little money and how few possessions you own, having a dog makes you rich.

LOUIS SABIN

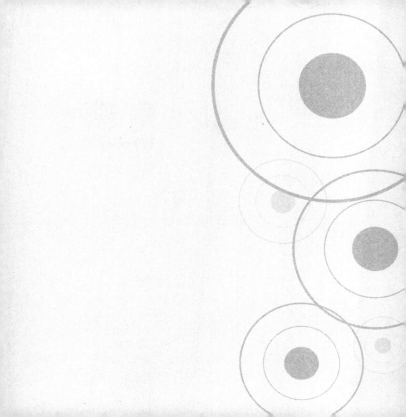